Progress
NOT
Perfection

First edition: 2020

ONE DAY
at a time

It works
if you
work it

GRATEFUL I'M
NOT
DEAD

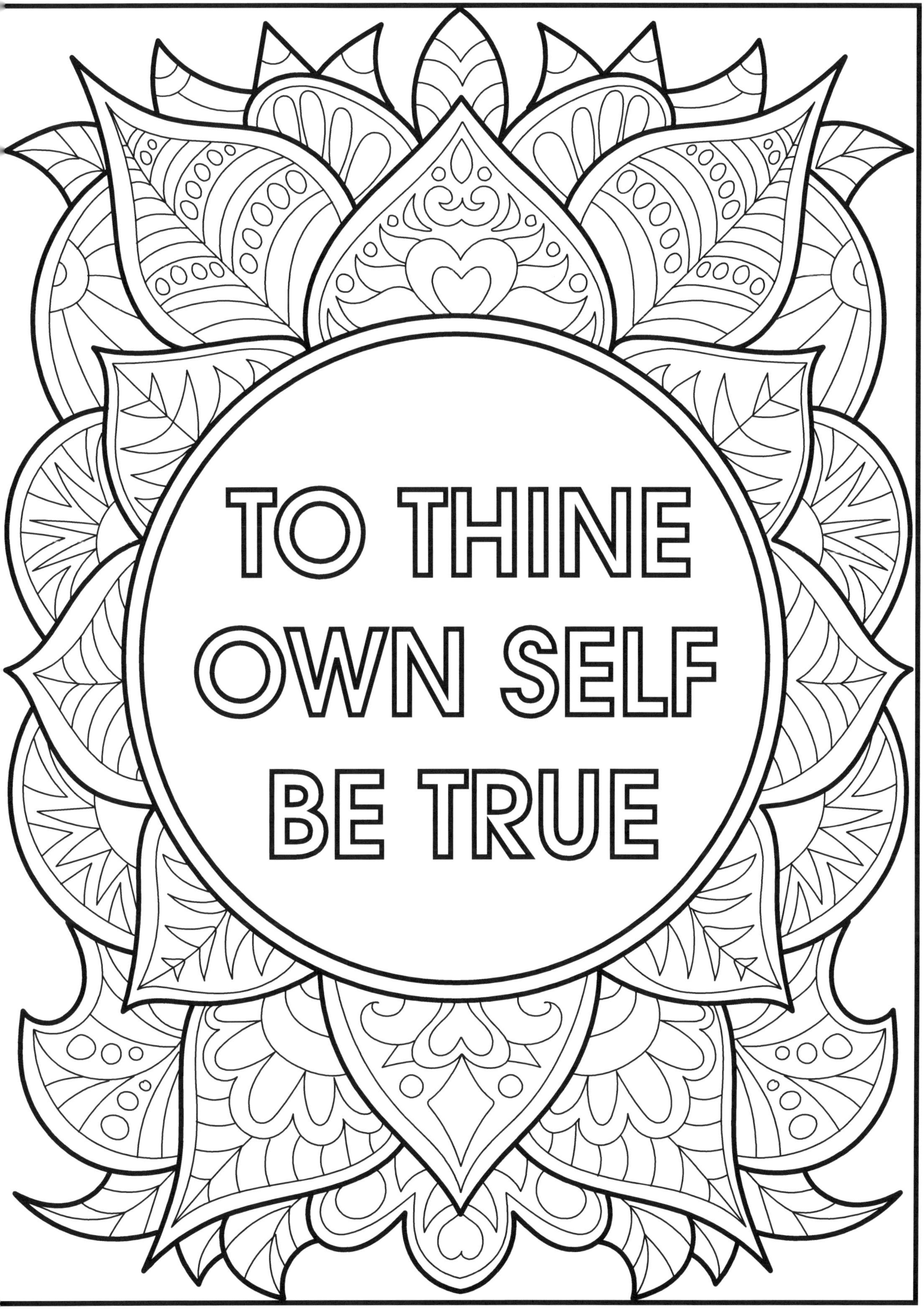
TO THINE
OWN SELF
BE TRUE

JUST
FOR
TODAY

Progress
not
Perfection

KEEP IT
simple
STUPID

F.E.A.R.
Face
Everything
And
Recover

Keep coming back

Talk
about
EVERYTHING.
Drink
about
NOTHING.

Thy will
not mine
be DONE

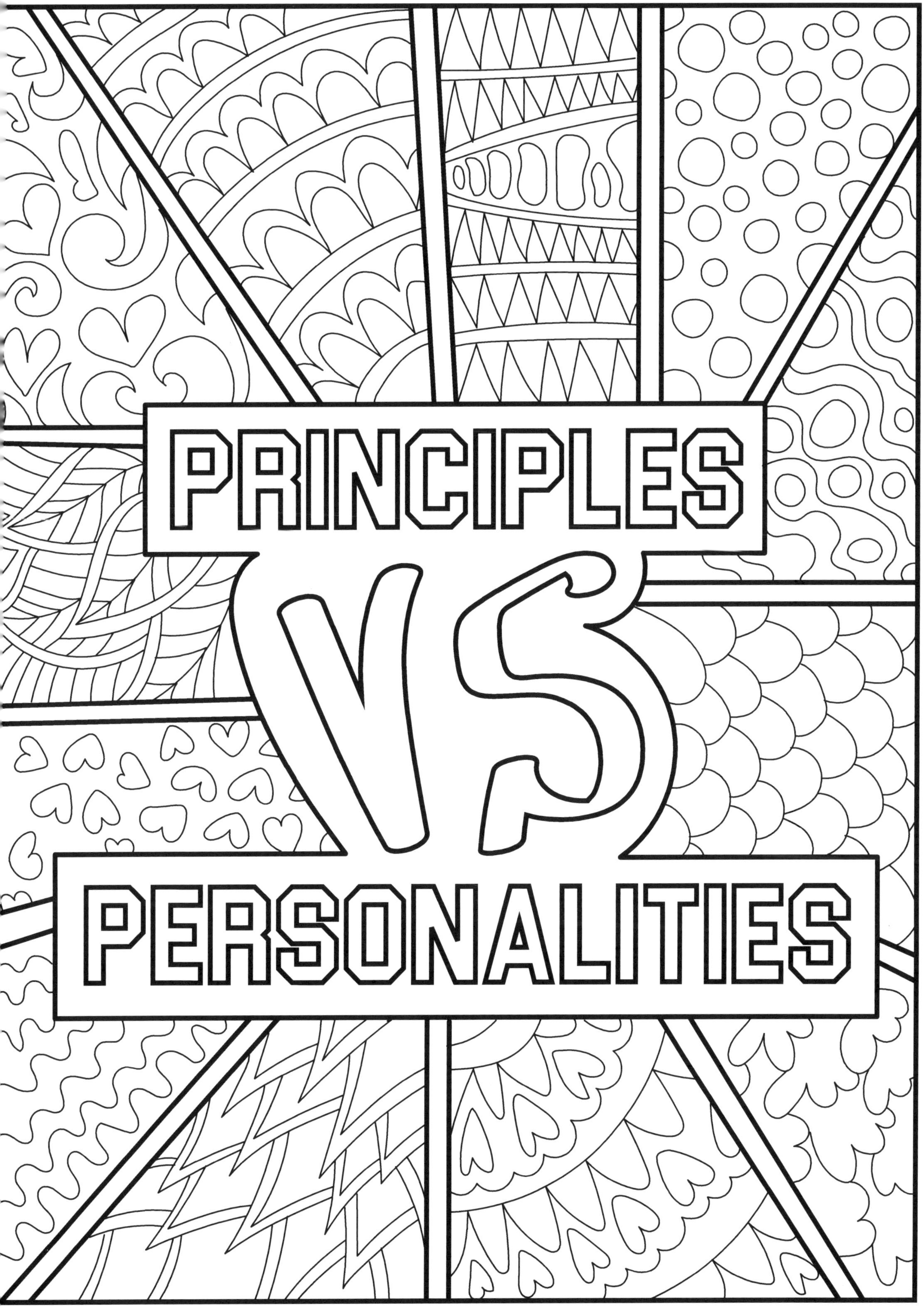
PRINCIPLES
VS
PERSONALITIES

ATTITUDE
OF
GRATITUDE

G.O.D.
Good
Orderly
Direction

ANGER
IS A LUXURY
I CAN'T
AFFORD

HUMILITY
IT'S
OK
TO BE ME

Happy joyous and free

Live
and let
Live

Problems
are solutions
in training

ANGER IS
ONE LETTER
AWAY FROM
DANGER

I'M EXACTLY
WHERE I
SHOULD BE

IF I'M NOT THE
PROBLEM THEN
THERE'S NO
SOLUTION

Don't take yourself so damn seriously

Meeting Makers make it

Stick with the winners

Today
IS THE
tomorrow
YOU WORRIED ABOUT
yesterday

We may be
powerless
but we're not
helpless

Surrender
IS NOT
a one time
THING

Easy does it
but do it

This too Shall pass

Made in the USA
Middletown, DE
29 November 2024

65628609R00035